God's
CHARACTER

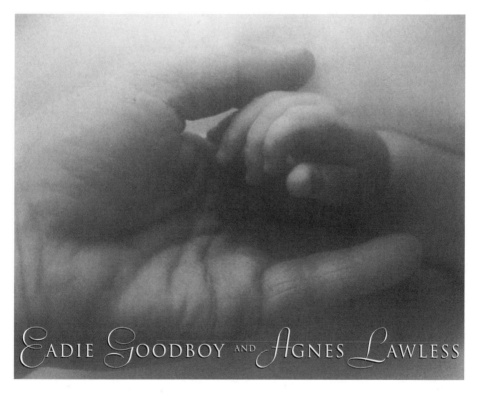

EADIE GOODBOY AND AGNES LAWLESS

Gospel Light

AGLOW
INTERNATIONAL

PUBLISHING STAFF
William T. Greig, Publisher
Dr. Elmer L. Towns, Senior Consulting Publisher
Dr. Gary S. Greig, Senior Consulting Editor
Jill Honodel, Editor
Pam Weston, Assistant Editor
Kyle Duncan, Associate Publisher
Bayard Taylor, M.Div., Senior Editor, Theological and Biblical Issues
Barbara LeVan Fisher, Cover Designer
Debi Thayer, Designer
Eva Gibson, Contributing Writer

Aglow International is an interdenominational organization of Christian women. Our mission is to lead women to Jesus Christ and provide opportunity for Christian women to grow in their faith and minister to others.

Our publications are used to help women find a personal relationship with Jesus Christ, to enhance growth in their Christian experience, and to help them recognize their roles and relationships according to Scripture.

For more information about our organization, please write to Aglow International, P.O. Box 1749, Edmonds, WA 98020-1749, U.S.A., or call (425) 775-7282. For ordering or information about the Aglow studies, call (800) 793-8126.

CONTENTS

FOREWORD

When the apostle Paul poured out his heart in letters to the young churches in Asia, he was responding to his apostolic call to shepherd those tender flocks. They needed encouragement in their new life in Jesus. They needed solid doctrine. They needed truth from someone who had an intimate relationship with God and with them.

Did Paul know as he was writing that these simple letters would form the bulk of the New Testament? We can be confident that the Holy Spirit did! How like God to use Paul's relationship with these churches to cement His plan and purpose in their lives, and, generations later, in ours.

We in Aglow can relate to Paul's desire to bond those young churches together in the faith. After 1967, when Aglow fellowships began bubbling up across the United States and in other countries, they needed encouragement. They needed to know the fullness of who they were in Christ. They needed relationship. Like Paul, our desire to reach out and nurture from faraway birthed a series of Bible studies that have fed thousands since 1973 when our first study, *Genesis*, was published. Our studies share heart-to-heart, giving Christians new insights about themselves and their relationships with and in God.

God's generous nature has recently provided us a rewarding new relationship with Gospel Light Publications. Together we are publishing our Aglow classics, as well as a selection of exciting new studies. Gospel Light began as a publishing ministry much in the same way Aglow began publishing Bible studies. Henrietta Mears, one of its visionary founders, formed Gospel Light in response to requests from churches across America for the Sunday School materials she had written for the First Presbyterian Church in Hollywood, California. Gospel Light remains a strong ministry-minded witness for the gospel around the world.

Our heart's desire is that these studies will continue to kindle the minds of women and men, touch their hearts, and refresh spirits with the light and life a loving Savior abundantly supplies.

This study, *God's Character* by Eadie Goodboy and Agnes Lawless, will guide you in your quest to know your heavenly Father better and serve to mold your character to be more like His. I know its contents will reward you richly.

Jane Hansen
International President
Aglow International

INTRODUCTION

The new baby is presented to her relatives at a dinner party. Family members peer at her. Her features and expressions are scrutinized.

"Look at that darling nose!" declares her grandmother. "She definitely inherited it from our side of the family."

"Did you see her smile?" says an aunt. "She looks just like her dad."

As the baby grows, she becomes more and more like her father. Her appearance, mannerisms, expressions and behavior show that she is truly her father's daughter.

This is true not only in the physical realm but in the spiritual as well. Like any parent, our heavenly Father wants His children to resemble Him, and while He was on earth, Jesus was "the radiance of God's glory and the exact representation of his being" (Hebrews 1:3) and "the image of the invisible God, the firstborn over all creation" (Colossians 1:15).

As the adopted children of God, "we are heirs—heirs of God and coheirs with Christ" (Romans 8:17), and we "are being transformed into his likeness with ever-increasing glory" (2 Corinthians 3:18).

To grow increasingly like our Father, it is essential that we know what He is like. As we study the attributes, or the character, of God, we will learn to know Him better and become more and more like Him.

AN OVERVIEW OF THE STUDY

This Bible study is divided into four sections:

- A CLOSER LOOK AT THE PROBLEM defines the problem and the goal of the study.
- A CLOSER LOOK AT GOD'S TRUTH gets you into God's Word. What does God have to say about the problem? How can you begin to apply God's Word as you work through each lesson?

- **A Closer Look at My Own Heart** will help you clarify and further apply truth. It will also give guidance as you work toward change.
- **Action Steps I Can Take Today** is designed to help you concentrate on immediate steps of action.

You Will Need

- A Bible.
- A notebook. During this study you will want to keep a journal to record what God shows you personally. You may also want to journal additional thoughts or feelings that come up as you go through the lessons. Some questions may require more space than is given in this study book.
- Time to meditate on what you're learning. Give the Holy Spirit time to personalize His Word to your heart so that you can know what your response should be to the knowledge you are gaining.

HOW TO START AND LEAD A SMALL GROUP

One key to starting and leading a small group is to ask yourself, What would Jesus do and how would he do it? Jesus began His earthly ministry with a small group of disciples. The fact of His presence made wherever He was a safe place to be. Think of a small group as a safe place. It is a place that reflects God's heart, God's hands. The way in which Jesus lived and worked with His disciples is a basic small group model that we are able to draw both from direction and nurture.

Paul exhorts us to "walk in love, as Christ also has loved us and given Himself for us" (Ephesians 5:2, *NKJV*). We, as His earthly reflections, are privileged to walk in His footsteps, to help bind up the brokenhearted as He did or simply to listen with a compassionate heart. Whether you use this book as a Bible study, or as a focus point for a support group, a church or home group, walking in love means that we "bear one another's burdens" (Galatians 6:2, *NKJV*). The loving atmosphere provided by a small group can nourish, sustain and lift us up as nothing else does.

Jesus walked in love and spoke from an honest heart. In His endless well of compassion He never misplaced truth. Rather, he surrounded it with mercy. Those who left His presence felt good about themselves because Jesus used truth to point them in the right direction for their lives. When He spoke about the sinful woman who washed Jesus' feet with her tears and wiped them with her hair, He did not deny her sin. He said, "her sins, which are many, are forgiven, for she loved much" (Luke 7:47, *NKJV*). That's honesty without condemnation.

Jesus was a model of servant leadership. "Whoever desires to become great among you shall be your servant. And whoever of you desires to be first shall be slave of all" (Mark 10:43,44, *NKJV*). One of the key skills a group leader possesses is to be able to encourage the group members to grow spiritually. Keeping in personal contact with each member of the group, especially if one is absent, tells each one that he/she is important to the group. Other skills an effective group leader will develop are: being a good listener, guiding the discussion, and guiding the group to deal with any conflicts that arise within it.

Whether you're a veteran or brand new to small group leadership, virtually every group you lead will be different in personality and dynamics. The constant is the presence of Jesus Christ, and when He is at the group's center, everything else can come together.

YOU'RE INVITED!

To grow...

To develop and reach maturity; thrive; to spring up; come into existence from a source;

with a group

An assemblage of persons gathered or located together; a number of individuals considered together because of similarities;

To explore...

To investigate systematically; examine; search into or range over for the purpose of discovery;

new topics

Subjects of discussion or conversation.

Meeting on

Date _____ Time_____

Located at

Place _____

_____

Contact _____

Phone _____

Note: Feel free to fill in this page and photocopy it as an invitation to hand out or post on your church bulletin board.

- One -

BORN TO BE LIKE HIM

"You look just like your mother," an old friend exclaims as you slip into a navy blue blouse that brings out the blue of your eyes.

As the years roll by, you catch yourself acting more and more like her, too. You roll out pie dough, then rub the back of your hands on the thighs of your blue jeans. Your daughter runs to you when she's scraped her knee—you kiss the owie and make it well.

You realize then that it's in the genes—like mother, like daughter. And the process has only just begun.

1. Which of your parents are you most like? In what ways are you like your mother or your father?

   Take one characteristic that you admire about her/him and tell how you would like to see it developed in your own life.

A Closer Look at the Problem

When we became Christians, we were born into the spiritual family of God. At our new birth, He planted His Spirit within us. Then comes the process of slowly transforming us into the likeness of His Son Jesus.

But how can this be? You may wonder. God is vast and wonderful and His characteristics are vast and wonderful too. He even says in Isaiah 55:8,9 that His thoughts and ways are beyond our understanding.

Yes, great mystery surrounds the nature of God. Yet God is knowable. Paul said that because He is, we can be like Him for we "are being transformed into his likeness with ever-increasing glory" (2 Corinthians 3:18). God literally accomplishes a life-changing transformation for those who truly believe in Jesus Christ.

But how does it happen? Can frail imperfect humans really be like Him? If so, how can we be participants with Him in this amazing transformation?

One of the things we can do is study God's characteristics or attributes as revealed in His Word—His mercy, faithfulness, love and many other attributes all express who He is and how we should respond to Him.

This chapter will help us gain insight into how we are slowly being transformed. We'll delve into Paul's epistles, then go with Moses to the top of the mountain to be with God. Together we will discover more about how we can be like Jesus.

A Closer Look at God's Truth

THE PROCESS OF CONFORMATION

2. Perhaps no writer was more aware of the process of being conformed into the image of Christ than was the apostle Paul. Read Romans 8:28,29. What is one of God's great purposes in redeeming us?

3. Read Philippians 1:6. How long does this process of conforming take?

4. Read 1 Corinthians 2:12-16 and 6:11. What part does the Holy Spirit have in this conforming?

5. Read Romans 8:14-18. What are those who are led by the Spirit called (see vv. 14,16)?

What is the ultimate goal of being led by the Spirit and conformed to Christ's image (see v. 17)?

What must we experience before sharing His glory (see vv. 17,18; also Hebrews 5:8)?

Describe the kind of suffering you think is referred to in Romans 8:17,18 and in Philippians 3:10.

What kind of suffering have you experienced? Could any of it be described as "sharing in his sufferings"?

DESIGNED TO REIGN

6. If you have suffered with Christ, what responsibilities do you think you were (or are) being trained for?

Complete the following verses:

"If we _____, we will also _____ with him" (2 Timothy 2:12).

"You have made them to be a _____ and
_____ to _____ our
God, and they will _____ on the earth"
(Revelation 5:10).

Not only will Christ reign as King of kings, but we, too, are designed to reign with Him. Now we can better understand why we experience sufferings and trials.

During our years on earth, the Holy Spirit is maturing and equipping us to rule. If royal heirs to secular kingdoms are placed in schools demanding much study and highly disciplined training, how much more do the children of God need training to be spiritually strong and to wisely rule others?

7. When trials come into your life, do you feel that you are being punished or that you are being equipped to rule with Jesus? Explain your answer.

If you realized that trials were God's loving way of maturing and training you for His great purposes, would it make a difference in your attitude? How?

Can you see through present or past trials and recognize that all things are working together for your good (see Romans 8:28)? Share a particular time of testing that you can say God has worked together for good in your life. Explain how.

CHOOSING HIS GLORY

8. Read Romans 12:1,2. What one thing must we do in order to grow in Christ's likeness?

Do you love and trust God enough to obey these verses in Romans? If not, what prevents you from doing so?

What would it take for you to do this?

9. Read 2 Corinthians 3:18. Who does the actual transforming?

What part do you think believers might have in this process?

Paul took it for granted that true Christians reflect something of God's glory. However, even as we cannot earn our salvation, neither can we do anything on our own to grow into that glory. The Holy Spirit does the work, but we must offer ourselves and be available to Him. One way we can do this is to spend time with God.

The next Scripture passage takes us into the Old Testament.

10. Read Exodus 34:1-10,27-35. According to verse 2, what action was Moses to take?

What did God reveal to Moses about Himself (see vv. 6,7)?

How did Moses respond (see v. 8)?

How long was Moses alone with God (see v. 28)?

In what way was Moses changed by his time with God (see v. 29)?

How do Moses' actions compare to what we are entreated to do in Romans 12:1,2?

11. Read 2 Corinthians 3:7-11, then reread Exodus 34:29-35. Compare the glory Moses received with that which we have available in Christ.

Why don't we always have His radiance on our faces?

Reread 2 Corinthians 3:18. To what attributes of God's character (mentioned in 3:7-11) is Paul referring in this verse?

What qualities of the Lord's character would you like to see reflected in your life?

A Closer Look at My Own Heart

Prayerfully read through the following questions. They are designed to help you evaluate your relationship with Jesus.

12. Do I know that I belong to God? If not, will I receive Him now as my Savior and Lord?

Am I comfortable in God's presence? Do I converse freely with Him in prayer?

Is my relationship with the Father one of close, trusting intimacy or does

He seem vague and far-off? If the latter, what can I do to improve my relations with Him?

Do I look forward to spending time with the Lord? Is time spent in prayer and Bible reading a pleasure to me?

How much time do I actually spend with God alone each day?

How much time do I devote to worship?

Prayer?

Bible reading and meditating on His Word?

ALONE WITH GOD

You may not be able to spend 40 days and nights alone with God the way Moses did, but you can take time to be with God. Even Jesus spent time alone with His heavenly Father when He was here on earth.

13. Read Mark 1:35; 6:46; Luke 3:21; 5:16; 6:12; 9:28; 11:1. Why was it important for Him to do this?

How will time spent alone with the Lord shape you into the image of Christ?

Action Steps I Can Take Today

Prayerful time alone with God in His Word is a living encounter with Jesus Christ Himself—a time when you meet Him face-to-face. Without spending time in His presence you cannot grow in likeness to Him.

14. Will you make a commitment to listen and talk to Him this week? If your answer is yes, you are encouraged to ask a friend to keep you accountable. Check in with your friend several times this week.

15. Write Psalm 17:15 on a 3x5-inch card and put it beside your bed. Make the verse a part of your evening prayer as you end each day this week with Him.

- *Two* -

 # THE MERCY OF GOD

What is mercy? Basically mercy means kindness. The same Hebrew word has been translated in various ways: "love," "loving-kindness," "compassion" and "mercy."

Someone has expressed this mercy in a prayer poem:

> Teach me to feel another's woe,
> To hide the fault I see;
> That mercy I to others show
> That mercy showed to me.
> —Author unknown

A Closer Look at the Problem

In spite of our sins and failures, God's mercy is boundless and ours for the asking. However, we must meet certain conditions before we receive His mercy. We also have a responsibility to pass His mercy on to others.

The goal of this lesson is to help us develop a deepened comprehension of God's mercy and ourselves as channels of that mercy.

1. Reread the above poem. As you do, substitute kindness or one of the words commonly translated as "mercy" for the word "mercy."

A Closer Look at God's Truth

IN PRAISE OF GOD'S MERCY

2. Read 2 Samuel 24:14. What attribute of God is described here?

   How is it described?

3. Read Exodus 34:6,7. How does God describe Himself?

4. Read the following scriptures and describe God's mercy or love found in them.

   Psalm 57:10

   Psalm 136:1

   Ephesians 2:4

   James 5:11

Either summarize the truth in these verses into two or three sentences, or use phrases from the verses to write a praise song to the Lord.

5.   Read Lamentations 3:22,23. Even when we fail Him, what comfort do we have in Him? Fill in the blanks:

"Because of the LORD's great _____ we are not consumed, for his _____ never fail. They are new every morning."

Write the dictionary definition of "compassionate":

GOD'S MERCY TO HIS PEOPLE

We have seen that God is merciful and have read some verses that describe His mercy. Now let us see how His mercy is manifested to us and to all mankind.

6.   Recall a situation in your life when God's mercy was evident to you. What did God do? How did you respond?

7.   Read Nehemiah 9:16,17,29-31. How did God evidence His merciful compassion to the Israelites when they sinned against Him?

According to Titus 3:5, how does God manifest His mercy to us? Fill in the blanks: "He saved us, not because of _____things we had done, but because of his _____."

RECEIVING GOD'S MERCY

8. We know we need God's mercy, but how can we receive it? To whom does He show His kindness and compassion? Read the following verses and list the phrases that tell to whom God extends His mercy.

Exodus 20:6

2 Chronicles 6:14

Psalm 32:10

Psalm 86:5

Psalm 103:11

Proverbs 28:13

Hebrews 4:16

Which one of these verses is most meaningful to you concerning God's mercy and why?

BECOMING CHANNELS OF GOD'S MERCY

9. Not only do we know God's mercy for ourselves, but we in turn should show mercy to others. Read Matthew 5:7 and Luke 6:36. As a result of God's mercy to us, by what principle does Jesus instruct us to live?

    Why does He call the merciful blessed?

10. Read Colossians 3:12. While we are being conformed to the image of Christ, Paul tells us to "put on" certain qualities. The first Christlike quality he mentions is compassion. What does compassion mean to you?

    Give an example of someone who shows compassion to others. Tell what that person has done. Try to define the attitude in which it was done.

11. Read Proverbs 19:17 and Zechariah 7:9,10. In what ways were God's people to show mercy to others?

    According to Zechariah 7:11-14, when the Israelites failed to practice such mercy, what was the result?

    Do you see yourself as a judging or a merciful person?

Do you perceive judging as a sin or a right? Why?

12. Read Deuteronomy 14:28,29 and 24:19. To whom does God expect His people to be merciful?

What will His people who are merciful receive as a result?

Why is it so important to God that we show mercy?

13. Read 2 Corinthians 1:3,4. How is God described to His own children?

For what purpose does He comfort us in our trouble?

A Closer Look at My Own Heart

We are never more beautiful or Christlike than when we reflect the mercy of God in practical ways. Read Luke 10:25-37. In this parable Jesus gives an example of showing mercy in a practical way. Traditionally, the Jews and Samaritans hated each other. Therefore, the Jews must have been rankled that Jesus made a Samaritan the hero of this story.

Read verses 33-35 carefully, noting the compassion of the Samaritan toward one who was his national enemy. The money he paid for the injured man's lodging was probably adequate for two months.

14. In verse 37, what does Jesus say to the lawyer (and to you)?

How do you think you would react if Jesus told you to show the same quality of mercy to someone you hated? Write about it in your journal.

As you do, interact with the following statement: It is only by choosing to obey God's Word and by the power of the Holy Spirit that we can extend this kind of mercy to someone who has deeply wounded us or someone we love.

Ask God to help you select a verse from His Word to explain your answer.

Action Steps I Can Take Today

15. Have you taken the mercy of God for granted? Begin now to praise Him daily for His mercy to you. Write Psalm 86:15 on a 3x5-inch card and place it beside your bed. Make it your morning praise song each day this week.

16. Ask God to make you a channel for His mercy to flow to others. Ask Him to show you a particular person to whom you can be a channel of God's comfort. Pray for that person each day this week. Ask God to show specific ways that you can comfort/encourage this person.

Three

THE FAITHFULNESS OF GOD

God is faithful. We can…

- count on Him to keep His Word;
- rely on Him to make good on His promises;
- depend on Him to do what He has said He will do;
- trust Him to remain loving and loyal to us no matter what.

God is a person upon whom we can rely absolutely. What a wonderful Friend He is!

1. Does this describe the God you know? If not, why not?

A Closer Look at the Problem

GOD'S FAITHFULNESS IN AN UNFAITHFUL WORLD
We live in a world where faithfulness is rare. Materialism is on the rise, families are in trouble, and divorce is rampant.

Lisa had a husband, two sons and a successful business she ran from her home and a cabin in the woods. Listen to what she has to say:

"Even though I had it all, it didn't satisfy. My husband bored me—I quit trying to meet his needs. The boys and I stopped going to church—I was too busy anyway. Eventually I had an affair. It didn't last long, but it was long enough for me to lose my husband and family. Even my business.

"I know now that I had a lot to learn about commitment and faithfulness. Or maybe I did know but just didn't want to put it into practice.

"Whatever, I'm just glad God hasn't given up on me. He's right there beside me, helping me get my life back on track. It hasn't been easy, but one thing I know. God is faithful."

Lisa has learned about faithfulness the hard way. Her words attest to the faithfulness of her Lord.

This lesson will help us understand more about the trustworthiness of our Lord. And that isn't all. It will also show us how to respond in faithfulness to Him and to others.

A Closer Look at God's Truth

Let's begin by looking first at the Bible and seeing what God has to say about Himself.

2. Read Revelation 19:11. What is Christ as the rider of the white horse called?

3. In the following references, how does God show Himself to be faithful?

    Deuteronomy 32:4

    Isaiah 25:1

    Isaiah 49:7

The words "faithful" and "faithfulness" come from a Hebrew word that means "to prop or support."[1] When applied to a person, it means one on whom we can safely rely. In Greek "faithful" may be translated "trustworthy."[2]

GOD'S FAITHFULNESS DESCRIBED

4. Read the following scriptures describing the extent of God's faithfulness. Then write the reference beside the correct description:

Psalm 33:4   Psalm 36:5   Psalm 89:2   Psalm 89:8   Psalm 146:6

_____   It is established in the heavens.

_____   His faithfulness reaches to the skies.

_____   He remains forever faithful.

_____   He is faithful in all He does.

_____   His faithfulness surrounds Him.

How can these verses give you a sense of security?

We have seen that God's faithfulness is boundless. Therefore, we can confidently rely on Him for all our physical, mental and spiritual needs.

Now let us see how God manifests His faithfulness to His children.

GOD'S FAITHFULNESS IN ACTION

5. Read the following verses and tell how God shows His faithfulness to us:

Deuteronomy 7:9

1 Kings 8:56

Psalm 119:89,90

Hebrews 10:23

Hebrews 10:36-38

God is always faithful in keeping His covenants and promises to His people. Let us look at other ways in which His faithfulness is expressed toward us.

6. Read 1 Peter 4:19. What should those who suffer do?

When we commit ourselves to God in times of trial, He shows His faithfulness to us by delivering us in His time and way.

7. From your personal experiences and your present knowledge of God, has He always been faithful to you? Why or why not?

If you were encouraging someone to become a Christian, could you describe God as One on whom it is safe to totally lean? What would you say?

8. Read 1 Corinthians 10:13. How are we assured that we are not the only ones who are being tempted or tested?

How does God show His faithfulness to us?

What does He provide for us?

The word translated "temptation" or "testing" means "a putting to proof or an experience."[3] It implies going through adversity, a time of testing. In His faithfulness and by His grace, God does not allow His suffering children to endure more than they can handle.

How can this knowledge of God's faithfulness give you comfort in your trials?

9. Read Psalm 119:75. In what ways does God here show His faithfulness?

10. Read Hebrews 12:6,10. What does God do to those He loves and accepts as His children?

What is God's purpose for disciplining us?

Share a trying experience that made you depend more on God and worked for your good.

11. Read Lamentations 3:22,23 and fill in the blanks: God's compassions never _____. "They are _____ every morning; _____ is your _____."

12. Read 2 Timothy 2:13. When we are faithless to God, what do we know about His relationship to us?

Why is this so?

What does this tell you about the nature of God? Does it give you a greater desire to be faithful to Him?

13. Read 1 John 1:9. If we confess our sins, what will He do?

What else is God faithfully doing for us? Draw lines from the descriptions to the correct verses.

He strengthens and protects us.   1 Corinthians 1:8,9

He keeps us strong to the end.   1 Thessalonians 5:23,24

He sanctifies us until He comes.   2 Thessalonians 3:3

We observe the faithfulness of God in nature by the changing seasons, through history in fulfilled covenants and promises, and by experience. We see it in the Bible—the written expression of God's faithfulness to us.

14. Read Psalm 119:86; 1 Timothy 1:15 and Revelation 21:5. Why can we totally rely upon the Word of God?

A Closer Look at My Own Heart

BECOMING HIS FAITHFUL REPRESENTATIVES

We have seen that God is faithful and manifests that attribute to us in many ways. But He not only is faithful Himself; He wants us, as His representatives on earth, to be faithful, too.

15. Read the following verses, then describe ways in which we are expected to practice faithfulness:

2 Kings 12:15

2 Chronicles 34:12

Proverbs 11:13

Luke 16:10-12

Acts 17:11

1 Timothy 3:11

3 John 5

Analyze your faithfulness alongside the verses you have just read. Which areas are strong in your life?

Which areas need to grow?

What steps can you take now that will encourage your faithfulness to increase?

16. Even though God has called us to faithfulness, there are times when we do not know how to make this a reality. God understands our hearts. That's why His Word abounds with encouragement for us to continue on. Read the following verses and answer the questions:

Revelation 2:10—How long are we to remain faithful?

What will be our reward for faithfulness?

Proverbs 28:20—What will be a result of faithfulness in our daily lives?

Psalm 101:6—Who is God looking at?

Who will minister to the end?

17. Use the following questions to help you discern areas of need in your life:

    a.   When affliction comes, what attitude do I need in order to mature spiritually?

    b.   How can I be faithful even in small matters?

    c.   Am I ready to read and meditate on God's Word daily? What do I need to do to enable me to be faithful in my personal time with Him?

    d.   Remember, when friends disappoint you, God remains faithful to you. How can you return godlike faith to them?

Action Steps I Can Take Today

18. God desires that we respond to His faithfulness. Read Psalm 40:10 and 89:1. Respond to these scriptures by sharing a specific example of God's faithfulness to you. Then turn it into a song as the psalmist did in Psalm 78.

Notes:

1. James Strong, LL.D., S.T.D., *The New Strongs's Exhaustive Concordance of the Bible* (Nashville, Tenn.: Thomas Nelson Publishers, 1984), #539.
2. Ibid., #4301.
3. Ibid., #3986.

- Four -

THE GOODNESS OF GOD

A loving father provides for his children. He not only supplies them with a home, food, and clothing, but also, if possible, sets aside money for their future needs.

Just so, our heavenly Father shows His goodness to us by providing material and spiritual blessings as well as riches in heaven.

A Closer Look at the Problem

But sometimes, especially when difficulties come, it is possible to doubt the goodness of God.

1. Which of the following circumstances have you experienced? Put a check beside the ones that made you wonder if God was truly good.

    ❑ financial setback   ❑ death of a loved one
    ❑ illness   ❑ family dissension
    ❑ church conflict   ❑ housing problem
    ❑ loss of job   ❑ other _____

In spite of either our feelings or our circumstances, God's Word stands firm. God is good.

In this lesson we will see how His goodness is manifested to us materially and spiritually. We'll also see what our response to that goodness should be and how we can pass it on to others.

Yes, God is good, even during difficult times. It's something we need to remember and rejoice in.

A Closer Look at God's Truth

AN OVERVIEW OF GOD'S GOODNESS

2.   Read the following verses and complete the sentences:

2 Chronicles 7:3—By His very nature, God is _____.

Psalm 31:19—God's goodness is _____.

Psalm 145:9—The Lord is _____.

How have you seen the goodness of God expressed in the daily circumstances of your life? Give a specific example.

MATERIAL BLESSINGS

3.   The Lord manifests His goodness, first of all, by giving us material blessings. Read the following verses and note how these blessings are described:

Psalm 21:3

Psalm 65:11

Psalm 68:9,10

Jeremiah 33:1,9

4. Read Matthew 5:45 and Acts 14:17. What material blessings does the Lord give us in His goodness?

   What material blessings has God given you? Make a list of them in your journal.

SPIRITUAL BLESSINGS

5. The Lord not only gives us bountiful material blessings but spiritual blessings as well. Look for these as you read Isaiah 63:7,9 and complete the blanks:

   The prophet Isaiah said, "I will tell of the _____ of the LORD, the _____ for which he is to be praised...yes, the many _____ _____ he has done for the house of Israel. In all their distress he too was _____, and the angel of his presence _____ them. In his love and mercy he _____ them; he _____ them up and carried them all the days of old."

6. Read Psalm 31:19-24. In verse 19, notice that God has stored up good things for those who _____ Him.

   Summarize some of the other ways God shows His goodness to us:

   verse 20a

verse 20b

verse 21

verse 23

What other spiritual blessings have you received, including special people in your life?

How can you then respond (see v. 24)?

Like a loving earthly father, God is storing up wonderful things for us in heaven and here on earth as we walk with Him. The word "bestow" in verse 19 literally means "to do or make."[1] It is translated "wrought" in some versions. This idea is to make or do some things systematically and habitually.

It is God's practice to do good things for His children, like an earthly father who builds a go-cart for his son or a mother who paints lovely T-shirts for her daughter. God not only habitually does good things for us, He also does them systematically according to His time schedule and perfect plan.

Our response should be one of reverence and trust.

Since the beginning of time, "No eye has _____ , no ear has _____ , no mind has _____ what God has for those who _____ him" (1 Corinthians 2:9).

In His goodness, God is preparing something for us so beyond our fondest dreams that we cannot even imagine what it will be like. No wonder we sing, "God is so good!"

EXPERIENCING FULL SATISFACTION

In this section, we want to look more in depth at another spiritual blessing God gives us out of His goodness—satisfaction. Often we try to find our satisfaction in earthly things. God shows us in His Word that it won't work.

7. Read Psalm 107:9 and Luke 1:53. What is the main prerequisite to being satisfied with God's goodness?

8. Read Psalm 81:8-16. Note some further conditions on our part for true satisfaction. We are to:

   verse 8

   verse 9

   verse 10

   verse 13

   What results does God then promise us?

   verse 10b

   verse 14

   verse 16

9. Read Isaiah 55:1-3. What is our spiritual condition apart from God (vv. 1,2a)?

   What can we do to change this condition (v. 1)?

How can we partake of God's food and drink (v. 2b)?

10. Read Psalm 103:5. What is the result of being satisfied with God's goodness?

Time spent with God in His Word and in prayer not only brings satisfaction but rejuvenation in body, soul and spirit. In the first part of this Bible study, we saw His goodness described. Then we saw how His goodness is made known to us materially and spiritually. Next we will see how we can respond to His goodness and how we can pass that goodness on to others.

REMEMBERING GOD'S GOODNESS

11. Read Psalm 103:1-5. What did David tell his soul (see v. 1)?

In the light of God's goodness, what are we not to do (see v. 2)?

What are these benefits? Draw lines to match the benefits with the verses in Psalm 103:

Redemption from the pit   verse 3a

Satisfaction with good things   verse 3b

Forgiveness of sins   verse 4a

Healing of diseases   verse 4b

Crowning with love and compassion   verse 5

REJOICING IN GOD'S GOODNESS

12. The Israelites expressed their attitude toward the goodness of God by worshiping Him (see 1 Kings 8:66). How can we follow their example?

Read Psalm 136:1. What are we to do?

How often do you rejoice in God's goodness?

Do you give God thanks at times other than your regular prayer time? Tell about when and how you do it.

SHOWING GOD'S GOODNESS TO OTHERS

13. Read the verses, then write after each reference how you can evidence God's goodness to others.

2 Corinthians 9:8

Galatians 6:9

Galatians 6:10

Hebrews 13:16

What are some practical ways we can show God's goodness to others? Be specific.

41

Read James 4:17. If we don't do good to others, what are we doing?

A Closer Look at My Own Heart

14. Use the following questions to help you prayerfully discern areas of need in your life.

How will understanding that God in His goodness is storing up good things for me and has a perfect plan for me, change my attitudes and lifestyle?

How does realizing God's goodness toward me affect my attitude toward suffering and trials?

Am I faithful about doing good to others? What can I do to improve?

Action Steps I Can Take Today

15. Think about the aspect of God's goodness that has been most meaningful to you in this study. How can your personal expression of that particular aspect make you more like Jesus? Write about it in your journal, then ask a friend to pray with you for this area and to keep you accountable about personally expressing God's goodness to others.

Note:
1. James Strong, LL.D., S.T.D., *The New Strongs's Exhaustive Concordance of the Bible* (Nashville, Tenn.: Thomas Nelson Publishers, 1984), #6466.

- Five -

THE WISDOM OF GOD

—⫷o/o/o⫸—

Our jet-black kitty likes to visit another cat across the street. However, we don't want her sauntering over there because we know she might get hit by a car. So we call her, go after her and scold her for her misdeed.

Kitty doesn't understand why she shouldn't visit her friend. She flips her tail and fusses and fumes. But in our higher wisdom, we know best.

Similarly, our heavenly Father knows best. His wisdom is infinitely higher than ours. Since He is all-wise, He knows all things in the past, present and future. He knows how to handle every situation.

A Closer Look at the Problem

OUR WISDOM OR GOD'S WISDOM?

1.   What are some of the ways that you have tried to gain wisdom?

2. Read Colossians 2:8. What dangers are involved in trusting the world's wisdom?

We are wise only when we reject our own poor wisdom and take His instead. This lesson will help us not to depend on our own reasoning but to trust God for the wisdom we need.

A Closer Look at God's Truth

We will begin by focusing on scriptures that describe the wisdom of God. You are encouraged to read the references slowly and prayerfully. Allow your heart to respond to the awesome greatness of His wisdom.

3. Read the following verses and describe the extent of God's wisdom and knowledge:

   Job 37:16

   Psalm 139:6

   Psalm 147:4,5

   Isaiah 40:28

   Daniel 2:22

4. Read Romans 11:33. Fill in the blanks to find out what Paul tells about God's wisdom.

   "Oh, the _____ of the _____ of
   the _____ and _____ of

God! How _____ His _____ and
His paths beyond tracing out!"

5. Read Isaiah 55:8,9. What does God say about His thoughts and ways as compared with ours?

   What picture does God use to describe how different His thoughts and ways are from ours?

   Since we cannot fully understand God's ways and thoughts, how then are we to pray?

GOD'S WISDOM MANIFESTED

Let's look at some of the ways God's wisdom is manifested to us.

6. Read Jeremiah 10:12. Fill in each blank with the correct word to see how God used His attribute of wisdom in creation:

   "God made the _____ by his _____;
   he founded the _____ by his
   and stretched out the _____ by
   his _____."

7. Read John 3:16 and Ephesians 1:7,8. What is the ultimate way God has shown His wisdom to us?

8. What does God know about us? Draw lines to match the phrases with the appropriate references:

Those who are His	Psalm 103:14
Our words before we speak	Psalm 139:4
Our way	Psalm 142:3
Number of our hairs	Matthew 6:8
How we are formed	Matthew 10:30
Our hearts	Luke 16:15
What we need before we ask	2 Timothy 2:19

How can these facts about God's knowledge of you help you to accept yourself?

JESUS, THE WISDOM OF GOD

9. In His life and ministry on earth, Jesus evidenced the wisdom of God. Read Isaiah 11:2. Fill in the blanks to summarize the qualities which the coming Messiah would have:

    "The _____ of the LORD will rest on him—the Spirit of _____ and of _____, the Spirit of _____ and of power, the Spirit of _____ and of the fear of the LORD."

Read Matthew 13:54 and Luke 2:40 and explain how Isaiah's prophecy was fulfilled.

10. Read Colossians 2:2,3 and fill in the blanks.

"That they may have the full riches of complete _____,
in order that they may know the mystery of God, namely,
_____, in whom are hidden all the
_____ of _____ and
_____."

We have seen that wisdom is an attribute of God the Father and His Son Jesus. But we also need to consider that He wants to give some of His wisdom to us, His children. Why do we need wisdom? What results will be obtained when we receive it?

11. Read James 3:17. Describe the quality of wisdom which we can receive from God.

How were these qualities evident in Jesus' life on earth? Give an example or two.

How are they evident in your life? Explain your answer.

How do you wish they were more evident in your life?

12. Read 1 Corinthians 1:18-31 and complete the following:

To Christians, Jesus is not only the _____ of God, but the _____ of God (see v. 24).

"The foolishness of God is _____ than man's _____, and the weakness of God is _____ than man's _____" (v. 25).

Why has God chosen the following?

Foolish things (v. 27)

Weak things (v. 27)

Lowly, despised, and "are not" things (v. 28)

What was His purpose in doing this (vv. 29,31)?

How has the Lord worked in your life to bring you to the place of boasting only of Him?

FOOLISH ENOUGH TO BELIEVE, WEAK ENOUGH TO TRUST

Now we know why God chose us. He did not choose us for our wisdom, might or nobility, but because we were foolish enough to believe and weak enough to trust in Him.

We realize now our need of God's wisdom, but how do we go about getting it? Let's look at three different ways spoken of in the Bible: reverencing God, asking Him for wisdom, and studying and obeying His Word.

REVERENCING GOD

13. Read Psalm 111:10. Fill in the blanks:

"The _____ of the LORD is the _____ of wisdom; all who follow his _____ have good _____."

Theologian J. I. Packer said, "Not till we have become humble and teachable, standing in awe of God's holiness and sovereignty, acknowledging our own littleness, distrusting our own thoughts, and willing to have our minds turned upside down, can divine wisdom become ours."[1]

ASKING GOD FOR HIS WISDOM

14. Read James 1:5,6. How do we receive divine wisdom?

What will God then do?

How do we ask for wisdom?

Do you find it easy to believe all that you have been taught in the Christian faith? If not, what hinders you?

Do you find the principles of faith easy to believe but difficult to live? Explain.

15. Read John 14:26 and 16:13. What is the role of the Holy Spirit in regard to God's wisdom?

What exactly do these verses tell us? Do you believe them? Why or why not?

Give a specific example of how the Holy Spirit has guided you into truth.

STUDYING AND OBEYING GOD'S WORD

16. Read Colossians 3:16. Fill in the blanks to find the source of wisdom.

"Let the _____ of Christ _____ in you richly as you _____ and admonish one another with all _____."

17. Read 2 Timothy 3:15,16. What kind of wisdom does the Bible give us?

For what is the Bible useful?

What is the purpose of Bible study?

OUR ALL-WISE, ALL-KNOWING GOD

Our all-wise God is fully aware of everything that happens to us. Even though Satan may bring difficulty our way, God still allows it for our good. He is able to see beyond our tears to the glory that will follow. He knows our thoughts, our fears, our desires, our circumstances.

18. Read Exodus 3:7-10. God said He had _____ the misery of His people in Egypt, had _____ their cries and was _____ about their suffering. He had come to
_____ .

19. Read Galatians 1:15,16. Even before the apostle Paul was born, God knew what he would become in later life. How do we know this?

How does 1 Peter 1:1,2 further emphasize this truth?

A Closer Look at My Own Heart

20. Take some time right now and meditate on Galatians 1:15,16 and 1 Peter 1:1,2. What emotions do you feel as you ponder these verses. Joy? Doubt? Great responsibility? Fear?

    Write your thoughts in your journal. Use the following questions to help you focus even more closely on the wisdom God has for you right now.

    a. Am I aware that God in His wisdom has a perfect plan for my life?

    b. Do I realize that everything that happens to me has the seal of God's wisdom on it?

    c. Do I understand why it is necessary to read God's Word and obey it?

    d. Will I seek to speak with God-given wisdom rather than with the wisdom of the world?

Action Steps I Can Take Today

21. Acquiring God's wisdom begins with prayer. Personalize Ephesians 1:17-19 into your own prayer. Change the "you" to "me" or "I," and the "your" to "my."

    Example: "I keep asking that the God of our Lord Jesus Christ, the glorious Father, may give [me] the Spirit of wisdom and revelation, so that [I] may know him better…"

22. Spend time praying this same prayer for someone else.

    Example: "I keep asking that the God of our Lord Jesus Christ, the glorious Father may give [insert name] the Spirit of wisdom and revelation, so that [he or she] may know him better."

    Another biblical prayer you can pray for yourself or others is Colossians 1:9-12.

Note:
1. J. I. Packer, *Knowing God* (Downers Grove, Ill.: InterVarsity Press, 1976), pp. 90-91.

– *Six* –

THE OMNIPOTENCE OF GOD

The fourth word in the Bible is the first mentioned name of God (see Genesis 1:1) in the Bible. The Hebrew for this name is *Elohim;* it means mighty, strong, prominent. Creative glory, power and Godhead fullness are connected with it, also the idea of omnipotence or governing power.

A Closer Look at the Problem

God is omnipotent. That means He is all-powerful. He has unlimited authority, power and influence. With Him, nothing is impossible.

We, however, are weak and powerless. Without God, we are nothing and can do nothing worthwhile. God wants us to realize this and to put our trust completely in Him, letting Him live and work through us.

A. B. Simpson, a middle-aged Presbyterian pastor, was physically sick, despondent and ready to quit the ministry. Then he heard someone sing, "Nothing is too hard for Jesus. No man can work like Him." After yielding himself to God, he was healed in body, mind and spirit and lived to do a great work for the Lord.

The goal of this chapter is to help us understand that we can ask for our Lord's power to do the impossible. His strength is activated within us through our weakness and dependence upon Him.

53

A Closer Look at God's Truth

Throughout the Old Testament we catch glimpses of God's almighty power in His various names. Those same names are unfolded in the person of Jesus Christ; they are further manifested in the revelation of who He is in the book of Revelation.

1. Read the following scriptures that show His power:

    Genesis 35:11—What does God call Himself in this verse?

    Psalm 91:1—What two names are used to refer to God?

    John 1:49—Who does Nathanael say Jesus is?

    Revelation 11:17—What is God called? Why is He called this?

The Hebrew word for almighty is *shadday*, derived from the word meaning "to be burly, powerful, impregnable."[1] In the New Testament, the Greek word for "almighty" is *pantokrater*, "the all-ruling one (as absolute and universal sovereign)."[2]

2. The following scriptures tell us more about our omnipotent God:

    Job 42:2—Of what was Job assured regarding God?

    Matthew 19:26—What did Jesus say about divine omnipotence?

3. God is able to do anything. As the God of infinite power, all things are possible with Him. How does the fact of God's power encourage you in your own circumstances?

GOD'S OMNIPOTENCE REVEALED IN NATURE

We have established that God is omnipotent. Now let us see how His power is further shown to us and our world.

4. The first way that God's omnipotence is revealed is in His control of nature. Read Psalm 33:6-9. Note various aspects of God's power in creation and complete the sentences:

Verse 6: By His Word He _____.

And by His breath He _____.

Verse 7: He gathers the _____.

The Living Bible paraphrases this verse: "He made the oceans, pouring them into his vast reservoirs."

And He puts the _____.

Verse 9: He spoke and _____.

He commanded, and _____.

5. Read Amos 4:13. List the things in nature over which God has control, as mentioned in this verse:

He forms the _____ and creates the
_____. He reveals His _____ to

man. He turns _____ to darkness. He treads the
_____ of the earth. His name is
the _____.

Why are there earthquakes, tornadoes and floods? Are they only indicators of God's power? Are they evidence of creation "out of control"?

Are these disasters sent to bring frightened people to salvation? What other possible reasons are there for these powerful displays of God's power?

Do we have the right or authority through prayer and the spoken word of faith to challenge or change weather conditions? Why or why not?

GOD'S OMNIPOTENCE REVEALED IN MANKIND

6. Not only is nature controlled by God's power, but men also are subject to His will. This also includes leaders of nations. Read Daniel 2:20,21 and 4:25. What belongs to the omnipotent God (see 2:20)?

    Note the things God is able to do to nations:
    "He changes _____ and _____.
    He sets up _____ and _____ them.
    He gives wisdom to the _____ and knowledge
    to the _____ " (Daniel 2:21).

    What are some other ways in which God controls nations?

If God sets up the heads of government, why should believers be involved in the political realm?

Do we even need to vote? Complete this statement: We vote because God uses men to…

GOD CONTROLS ANGELS BY HIS OMNIPOTENT POWER

7. Read Hebrews 1:14. What are angels called?

What are they commissioned to do?

What are some specific ways that angels minister to people today?

SATAN IS UNDER GOD'S OMNIPOTENT CONTROL

8. According to Job 1:12; 2:3-6, God told Satan he could go only so far in afflicting Job. Where did He draw the line?

In your view, is God always in complete control, or does the enemy's power sometimes come dangerously close to winning the battle?

SICKNESS IS UNDER GOD'S CONTROL

9. Read Matthew 8:14-17. How did Jesus minister to Peter's mother-in-law (vv. 14,15)?

Notice the extent of Jesus' healing ministry (v. 16). What Old Testament scripture did He fulfill (v. 17)?

GOD HAS POWER OVER DEMONS

10. Read Mark 1:23-28. How did Jesus deal with the unclean spirit?

    Why were people amazed at Jesus?

    As we grow more like Jesus, can we expect to exercise His kind of power over demons and sickness? Why?

GOD'S AUTHORITY OVER DEATH

11. Read John 10:17,18 and 11:43,44. What authority did Jesus have over death?

    How did He reveal this authority in the case of Lazarus?

OUR RESPONSE TO GOD'S OMNIPOTENCE

The first section of this lesson dealt with the fact of God's omnipotence. We next looked at the various ways God's power is shown. In this, our final section, we see how we are to respond to God's omnipotence.

12. First of all, God wants us to trust Him for impossible situations in our lives. Read Luke 1:26-55. What promise did God give Mary through the angel Gabriel (see v. 31)?

In verses 32 and 33, note the further aspects of this promise:

"He will be _____ and will be called the
_____ of the _____. The Lord
God will give him the _____ of his father David
and he will reign over the _____ of Jacob forever; his kingdom will _____ _____."

What honest question did Mary have (see v. 34)?

How was God's promise to be fulfilled (see vv. 35,36)?

The Holy Spirit would _____ _____ her and
the power of the Most High would _____ her.
Her child would be called the _____ of _____.
Elizabeth was going to have a _____ in her old
age and was in her _____ month of pregnancy.

What affirmation did Gabriel give Mary (v. 37)?

Verse 37 could be translated literally, "No word will be impossible of fulfill-
ment with God." The *Amplified Bible* says, "For with God nothing is ever
impossible and no word from God shall be without power or impossible of ful-
fillment."

God used an old woman, Elizabeth, to give birth to the prophet, John the
Baptist, and a virgin, Mary, to give birth to His Son Jesus. Elizabeth had a bar-
ren womb and Mary was a virgin. Both women faced impossible situations.
Yet out of these human impossibilities, God brought forth life, so that "no one
may boast before him" (1 Corinthians 1:29).

What was Mary's response to God's promise (see Luke 1:38)?

Share a promise God has given you and how He has fulfilled it. If it hasn't yet been fulfilled, explain how you believe He will do so in the future.

WE RESPOND IN DEPENDENCY ON GOD

13. The second way we can respond to God's omnipotence is by depending on Him entirely. Read 2 Chronicles 14. King Asa decided to follow the Lord fully. List the things Asa did in obedience to God in the following verses:

    verse 2

    verse 3

    verse 4

    verse 5

    What difficulty did Asa then face (v. 9)?

    Note Asa's powerful prayer in verse 11. Fill in the blanks:

    "LORD, there is no one like _____ to help the _____ against the _____.
    Help us, O LORD our God, for we _____ on you and in your _____ we have come _____ this _____ _____.
    O LORD, you are our _____; do not let man _____ against _____."

    How did God answer Asa's prayer (vv. 12,13)?

14. Read 2 Corinthians 12:9,10. The Lord said to Paul:

"My _____ is sufficient for you, for my
_____ is made perfect in _____."

What did Paul boast in?

For what reasons?

Paul said: "For when I am _____, then I am
_____."

Paul's statement is a paradox. What does he mean?

A Closer Look at My Own Heart

15. What is God saying to you? As you carefully read the following questions, ask God to show you what step He wants you to take in response to what you have learned about His omnipotence.

    a. How can the fact of God's omnipotence encourage me in my own difficult circumstances?

    b. Am I willing to believe and trust Him in what seems like impossible situations in my life? Why or why not?

c. Am I willing to depend upon His strength for my weakness? Why or why not?

d. How can my deepened understanding of my omnipotent God transform me more into the likeness of Jesus Christ?

e. In what ways can it change my attitude toward my weaknesses? The weaknesses of others?

Action Steps I Can Take Today

16. God is ever ready to put forth His power for you and those you love. Write a prayer to God expressing the areas in which you feel you need to experience His omnipotence.

Notes:

1. James Strong, LL.D., S.T.D., *The New Strongs's Exhaustive Concordance of the Bible* (Nashville, Tenn.: Thomas Nelson Publishers, 1984), #7703.
2. Ibid., #3841.

– Seven –

HE HOLINESS OF GOD

God is holy because He is absolutely pure, good and righteous. He has no sin; in fact, He hates sin. He is majestic and far above any of His creatures. See Hosea 11:9 and Isaiah 40:25.

A Closer Look at the Problem

Obviously, for us to be holy, as He is holy, would take an act of God. And it did. Hebrews 10:10 says, "we have been made holy through the sacrifice of the body of Jesus Christ once for all."

It is incredible that a holy God would share His holiness with us as He prepares us to live with Him in heaven. But He does.

Someone has well said, "Holiness means the most utter faithfulness, the most transparent truthfulness, the most decided honesty. It means every word you speak is perfectly true. You never flatter nor slander nor try to convey a false impression; you are all through alike in business, religion, and home life. It means you set yourself to bring every thought into harmony with the will of God. It means you do to others as you wish to be done by. It means the purest chastity."

This chapter will help us see that even though holiness seems lofty and unattainable to us, we can be holy as He is holy through the power of Jesus' blood.

A Closer Look at God's Truth

GOD IS HOLY

1. Let's begin our study by looking at scriptures that tell us about this attribute of God. Draw lines to match the phrases with the appropriate references:

   The Lord is holy.   Exodus 15:11

   God is majestic in holiness.   Psalm 22:3

   Holy is the Lord God Almighty.   Psalm 99:9

   He will show Himself holy.   Isaiah 5:16

   He is enthroned as the Holy One.   Revelation 4:8

JESUS IS HOLY

2. Jesus also has this attribute of holiness. What does the Bible say about Him? Draw lines to match the statements to the appropriate references:

   The holy and righteous One   Luke 1:35

   The holy One of God   Luke 4:34

   The holy servant Jesus   Acts 3:14

   The holy one to be born   Acts 4:30

Jesus did not become holy on earth; holiness was inherent in His nature. He shares the nature of God because He is God, the second person of the Trinity.

We have seen the fact of God's holiness in the scriptures we have read. But just what does the word *holy* mean? Ask God to give you understanding as you continue to look in His Word.

3. Why does Scripture say Christ was holy while on earth? Match each reference with the corresponding reason:

2 Corinthians 5:21   Hebrews 4:15   Hebrews 7:26   Hebrews 9:14   1 Peter 1:19

Christ had no sin.   _____

He offered Himself unblemished.   _____

He was holy, blameless, pure.   _____

He was a lamb without defect.   _____

He was without sin.   _____

What do the verses in questions 1 through 3 reveal about what it means to be holy? Try to explain in your own words the holiness of God the Father and His Son.

GOD DEMONSTRATES HIS HOLINESS TO MANKIND

4. How is the holiness of God manifested in the following verses?

Genesis 6:5-7

Psalm 5:4-6

Proverbs 15:9

John 3:16

GOD'S DESIRE FOR HIS PEOPLE

In this section of our study, we are going to see how God wants His people to be holy. He desires the same fellowship with men and women that He once had with Adam and Eve in the garden.

5. Read Isaiah 57:15. Even though God is holy and exalted, where may He be found?

   Who are the contrite and lowly in spirit?

6. Read Exodus 19:6 and Deuteronomy 7:6. How does God describe the Israelites?

7. Read Leviticus 19:2. What does God command His people?

Israel was the nation chosen by God to fulfill His purposes in the world. The nation of Israel was holy in the sense that it was set apart for God. But now God commands His people to act in a holy manner, to live holy lives.

8. Read Leviticus 18:3,4. By what means was Israel to exhibit holiness? Fill in the blanks:

"You must _____ _____ as they do in
_____ ...and you must
_____ as they do in the land of _____,
where I am bringing you. Do not _____ their
_____. You must _____ my
_____ and be careful to
_____ my _____."

God designed the moral, ceremonial and legal requirements so that Israel might be a holy people in deed as well as in fact.

9. Read 1 Peter 1:15,16. As God spoke to the Israelites centuries ago, what is His will for us today?

Why?

God does not say that we should be *as* holy as He is, for that is impossible, but He wants to share some of His holy nature with us.

How can we live holy lives in an unholy world?

CHOSEN TO SERVE

10. Read 1 Peter 2:9,10. List the five names God gives to those who believe on His Son. Compare these names with God's description of the Israelites in Exodus 19:6 and Deuteronomy 7:6 (see question 6).

11. Read Ephesians 1:4. What was God's plan for us when He chose us even before the creation of the world?

12. Read the following scriptures to learn more about how we are to serve our Holy God:

    Luke 1:74,75—Describe how God wants us to serve Him.

    Hebrews 12:14—What are we told to do in this verse?

    Why?

13. Read 2 Peter 3:10-12. Why is it important that we live holy lives?

    Read the following verses and give some results of being made holy (sanctified, when it applies to us, is another word for holiness).

    Matthew 5:8

    Acts 20:32

    Hebrews 2:11

    Hebrews 10:14

God is absolutely pure and holy. Therefore, He wants us to be holy, too. His desire is to have fellowship with us.

14. But how do we become holy? Read the following scriptures.

    Colossians 1:13—What has God done so we can be holy?

    1 John 1:9—What are we to do to become holy and pure?

    What then will God do?

CLEANSED TO SERVE

15. An example of the process of cleansing before service is found in an incident in the prophet Isaiah's life. Read Isaiah 6:1-8 and briefly describe the scene Isaiah saw.

    What were the seraphs saying about God?

    How did Isaiah feel about himself?

    How was his sin cleansed?

Once we see God in His awesome holiness, we see our wretched sinfulness. As we confess and forsake our sin, our fellowship with God is restored. Only when we are pure before Him, can we be of service to Him.

God has also given us His Word for our cleansing (Ephesians 5:26). We are spiritually cleansed as we read, study, meditate, memorize and obey God's holy Word, the Bible. It is our "bath," cleansing us from living in a defiled world.

16. Read 2 Peter 1:3,4. How has God equipped us to share in His divine nature?

"His _____ _____ has given us _____ we need for life and _____ through our _____ of him."

Note in verse 4 our means of becoming holy. Fill in the blanks:

"He has given us his very _____ and precious _____ , so that through _____ you may participate in the _____ _____ and _____ the _____ in the _____ caused by evil desires."

How have you experienced the power of God's Word to change you?

DISCIPLINED FOR HOLINESS

17. Read Hebrews 12:10,11. What is another method God uses to make us holy?

What will be the result of such training?

A Closer Look at My Own Heart

18. What is God saying to you? Carefully read the following questions. Ask God to show you what step He wants you to take in response to what you have learned about His holiness—about His expectation that you be His holy child.

a.   Am I a person of "unclean lips" (Isaiah 6:5)? What sins must I confess and forsake?

b.   Am I contrite and lowly in spirit (see Isaiah 57:15)? If not, will I confess my pride and ask for God's forgiveness?

c.   Do I regularly read and meditate on God's Word? Why or why not?

d.   Do I accept God's discipline in my life?

e.   Do I ask God to help me be holy in thought, word and deed?

Action Steps I Can Take Today

19. Complete the following sentence:
The step of action I feel God wants to me to take today in response to His holiness is…

Ask a friend to keep you accountable to what you have chosen to do.

20. Paraphrase 1 Thessalonians 5:23,24 into a prayer for yourself, then into a prayer for someone else. Claim the promise in verse 24 for both of you.

THE GRACE OF GOD

—◦◦◦—

Grace is often defined as God's unmerited favor toward humans. This simple acrostic helps us understand:

God's
Riches
At
Christ's
Expense

In His great kindness, God bestows benefits on undeserving mankind. A. W. Tozer said, "It is by His grace that God imputes merit where none previously existed and declares no debt to be where one has been before."[1]

A Closer Look at the Problem

To illustrate the magnitude of grace, Jesus told a story of a king who forgave a servant for a debt of millions of dollars. The servant, however, refused to extend grace to a fellow servant who owed him a few dollars. Instead of forgiving him, he had him thrown in jail (see Matthew 18:23-35).

73

We read this story and wonder: *How could the servant be so ungrateful and unforgiving when he had just been treated so graciously and mercifully?* But wait. Haven't we who have been forgiven by our Lord and Master acted in similar ways toward others? This chapter will not only show God's marvelous grace to us, but it will help us understand how we can extend that same grace to others.

A Closer Look at God's Truth

GOD IS GRACIOUS

1. In this first section, we will see that the Lord is gracious, a God of grace and compassion. Read Exodus 34:6 and complete the following sentence: God calls Himself the…

   Nehemiah said almost the same thing in Nehemiah 9:17. Give his description of God at the end of this verse.

JESUS IS GRACIOUS

2. Read John 1:14 and complete the following sentence:
   Jesus is full of…

   Read the following verses and describe this attribute of Jesus.

   Psalm 45:2

   Luke 2:40

   Luke 4:22

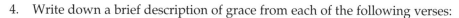

THE HOLY SPIRIT IS GRACIOUS

3. Read Hebrews 10:29. How is the Holy Spirit described?

GOD'S GRACE DESCRIBED

4. Write down a brief description of grace from each of the following verses:

    Romans 5:17

    2 Corinthians 12:9

    Ephesians 1:6

    Ephesians 1:7

    Put into your own words your understanding of this attribute of God.

    How does God's grace relate to you personally?

GOD'S GRACE IN ACTION

5. In this next section, we will see how God shows His grace to us. First of all, He saves us by His grace. Read Ephesians 2:1-3. What was our spiritual condition before His grace was exercised in our lives?

6. Read Titus 2:11. What does the grace of God bring?

   To how many people has grace been made available?

7. Read Titus 3:5-7. By what are we now justified?

   For what purpose?

8. Restate Ephesians 2:8,9 in your own words:

   What one ingredient must we have in order to appropriate God's grace for our salvation?

9. Exodus 33:19 in the *Amplified Bible* says: "And God said, I will make all My goodness pass before you, and I will proclaim My name, THE LORD, before you; for I will be gracious to whom I will be gracious, and will show mercy and loving-kindness on whom I will show mercy and loving-kindness."

   What fact concerning His sovereignty does God make clear?

   God is free to do as He pleases. He does not have to forgive our sins and save us, but He chooses to do so. How does this make you feel?

   Although God offers salvation to every person, why do only some receive it?

OTHER BENEFITS OF GRACE

10. Not only does God give us salvation by His grace, but He keeps giving many blessings to us throughout our earthly lives as Christians and on into eternity. What do the following verses tell us about the benefits other than salvation that God has given us by His grace?

2 Corinthians 8:9

2 Corinthians 12:9

Galatians 1:15

2 Thessalonians 2:16

2 Timothy 2:1

Hebrews 4:16

Hebrews 13:9

Can you remember a time when God gave you special grace during an especially difficult time? Tell about it.

11. Read Proverbs 3:34. To whom is God's grace given?

12. Read Ephesians 2:8,9. Why is it impossible for grace to operate in our lives if we try to earn it by works?

Grace then is the sovereign favor of God giving eternal life and showering blessings on those who do not earn or deserve it in any way.

What other benefits does the Lord give us as believers besides those mentioned above?

EXPRESSING GOD'S GRACE TO OTHERS

13. In this last section, we will see how we can show God's grace to others. Read 2 Corinthians 1:12. How does God want us to conduct ourselves?

What does Paul call us in Ephesians 2:10?

What were we created to do?

What kind of good works are we to do?

According to Philippians 2:13, who actually performs the good works through us?

14. Colossians 3:16,17 tells us good works are to be performed in Christ's name with a heart of thanksgiving. List the practical works you find here.

    According to John 15:8, what should be the end result of every good work?

15. Read Ephesians 4:32 and 1 Peter 4:9-11 and fill in the blanks. The first verse tells us how to minister the grace of God to others:

    "Be _____ and _____ to one another, _____ each other, just as in Christ God _____ you" (Ephesians 4:32).

    First Peter 4:10 says: "Each one should _____ whatever _____ he has _____ to _____ others, _____ administering God's _____ in its various forms."

    Verses 9 and 11 mention spiritual gifts that we can use to minister God's grace to others. What are the spiritual gifts mentioned?

    What is (are) your spiritual gift(s)? (Another verse concerning spiritual gifts is Romans 12:6-8.)

    How are you using your spiritual gift(s) to serve God's kingdom? Or if you are not using your spiritual gift(s), explain why.

16. Read 2 Corinthians 8:7 and 9:6-8. Paul urged the Corinthian believers to excel in what other grace?

We should give generously and _____.

How will God repay us when we give to those in need and in His service?

17. Read Ephesians 4:29. Name another way we can minister grace to others.

What gifts do you feel God has given you to minister to others?

How does it make you feel to think that He actually planned to give you these gifts before the world began?

A Closer Look at My Own Heart

18. Use the following questions to help you prayerfully discern areas in your own heart that need a touch of God's grace. Ask yourself:

a. Now that I understand the meaning of grace, what will my attitude be toward those I come in contact with each day?

b. Do the good deeds I do glorify God or myself? What is to be my attitude when doing them?

c. What attitude or behavior do I need to repent of in order that God's grace can be expressed in me?

Action Steps I Can Take Today

19. Write Ephesians 2:10 on a 3x5-inch card. Have you discovered the "good works" God has planned for you to do? Ask God to show you what they are. Be alert for opportunities to actually do those things He lays on your heart.

Note:

1. A. W. Tozer, *The Knowledge of the Holy* (New York: Harper and Row, 1961), p. 100.

Nine

HE LOVE OF GOD

Love is the essence of God's nature. Not only does He love, but He *is* love and the source of all love. His love is unchanging, free, spontaneous and undeserved.

In the New Testament, *agape*, one of four Greek words for love, is used over three hundred times. It expresses the highest type of love—divine love.

A Closer Look at the Problem

As we receive God's love, He wants us to love Him in return and then pass His love on to others. Someone has said:

> God is the source of love,
> Christ is the proof of love,
> Service is the expression of love.

But how do we experience this love? How do we pass it on to others? Not only will this chapter focus on the varied aspects of God's love, but it will help us understand how we can express that love to those around us.

1. Have you ever known or read about someone who demonstrated love by the things he or she said and did? Choose an incident that was memorable and be ready to tell about it.

A Closer Look at God's Truth

GOD'S LOVE

2. Read 1 John 4:8,16. What do these verses tell us about the character of God?

    God's love is described in various ways in Scripture. Write each reference beside the corresponding description of His love:

    Jeremiah 31:3   Romans 5:8   Ephesians 2:4   Ephesians 3:18

    _____ Great   _____ Immeasurable
    _____ Everlasting   _____ Sacrificial

THE FATHER'S LOVE

3. Let's discover how God manifests His love and to whom He shows it. From the following verses, list the recipients of the Father's love:

    Matthew 3:17

    John 3:16

    John 14:21

    John 16:27

    Romans 5:8

THE SON'S LOVE

4. As the second person in the godhead, Jesus has the same divine love as the Father. Whom does Jesus love? Draw lines from the persons He loves to the appropriate references.

    Believers   John 13:1
    His own disciples   John 14:31
    The Father   Ephesians 5:2
    The Church   Ephesians 5:25

EXPRESSIONS OF LOVE

5. From the following verses, write down some of the ways in which the Father shows His love to us:

    Isaiah 49:15

    Isaiah 63:9

    Zephaniah 3:17

    Ephesians 2:4,5

    Hebrews 12:6

    1 John 3:1

    1 John 4:9,10

TRUE LOVE IS SACRIFICIAL

6. Think about the deep love that you have for your own children, family members or a special friend, then reflect on the Father's sacrifice in giving His only Son to die for you. Would you be willing to allow your child or another person you love to go to a mission field in a foreign country if God directed him or her there? Why or why not?

7. Not only did the Father demonstrate His love in specific ways, so did the Son. Draw lines to match the statements with the appropriate references:

He makes us conquerors.	Luke 19:10
He became poor so we could be rich.	Romans 8:37
He disciplines us.	2 Corinthians 8:9
He came to save the lost.	Hebrews 7:25
He intercedes for us.	Revelation 1:5
He frees us from sin.	Revelation 3:19

Which item listed above is most meaningful to you right now? Why?

We have seen that God has the attribute of love and how He demonstrates it to us. How then do we respond to His love? Can we really love the way He loves?

The *Amplified Bible* says it like this: "Beloved, if God loved us so [very much], we also ought to love one another" (1 John 4:11).

8. What do the following verses say about how/why we can love others as God loves them?

Romans 5:5

1 Timothy 1:14

2 Timothy 1:7

9. How can we demonstrate our love for God? As you examine the following verses, write what He says to do and one practical way to show it in your daily life. Follow the first example:

	What to Do	**How to Show Love**
Psalm 97:10	*Hate evil*	*Stop lying*
Matthew 25:34-40		
1 John 2:15		
1 John 4:20,21		
1 John 5:3		

Put a check mark in front of the ones you are already participating in. Put an asterisk in front of the ones that you feel need to have a higher priority in your life.

LOVING OUR NEIGHBORS

10. Read Matthew 22:36-40. Summing up all the Law into two all-inclusive commands, Jesus told us to:

"Love the Lord your God with all your _____ and with all your _____ and with all your _____. This is the _____ and _____ commandment. And the second is _____ it: Love your _____ as _____."

Do you agree with the author who wrote this poem?

> To love the whole world
> For me is no chore;
> My only problem's
> My neighbor next door.
> —Author unknown

Why or why not?

LOVING OTHERS

11. Who else are we to love?

Matthew 5:44

John 15:12

Ephesians 1:15

Ephesians 5:25

1 Thessalonians 3:12

Titus 2:4

12. Notice the type of love God wants us to have for others. Draw lines from the descriptions of love to the correct references:

Active, true love	John 15:13
Deep love	Romans 12:9
Sacrificial love	Philippians 1:9
Abounding love	1 Peter 4:8
Sincere love	1 John 3:18

THE ULTIMATE GIFT

13. Read 1 Corinthians 13 and complete the following sentences:

Even if you give all your possessions to the poor and suffer martyrdom but don't have God's love, you _____.

C. I. Scofield says, "Gifts are good, but only if ministered in love."[1]

Review 1 Corinthians 13:4-7, then make a list of what love is or does and what it is not or does not do.

What Love Is/Does   What Love Is Not/Does Not Do

What gifts of the Spirit will remain forever (see v. 13)?

Which gift is greatest of all?

A Closer Look at My Own Heart

14. Read the following verses, then write down some of the ways in which you can show the love of God to others:

Galatians 5:13

Galatians 6:2

Galatians 6:10

Ephesians 4:32

Philippians 2:4

1 John 3:17,18

Carefully reread the list. After each reference write one or two specific ways you can put these commands into practice.

A THOUGHT TO REMEMBER
Someone has said:

> "Love is…
> Slow to suspect—quick to trust,
> Slow to condemn—quick to justify,
> Slow to expose—quick to shield,
> Slow to reprimand—quick to forbear,
> Slow to belittle—quick to appreciate,
> Slow to demand—quick to give,
> Slow to provoke—quick to help,
> Slow to resent—quick to forgive."

QUESTIONS TO PONDER

15. Do I love the Lord enough to give Him time each day as I read His Word, pray, praise and love Him?

16. Do I love Him enough to obey His commands?

17. Do I show His love to my family, friends and even those who do wrong to me?

18. What changes will I make in my life as a result of this study on the attributes of God?

A PRAYER TO PRAY

> Lord, You are holy, powerful and majestic, yet You invite me, Your child, to come into Your presence.
>
> I long to be conformed into Your image, to be like You, but I know now that this process has only just begun. It will only be perfected as I get to know You better and trust your Holy Spirit at work in me.
>
> Teach me Your Word. Help me to listen, obey and show Your love to others.
>
> I love You and praise You. You are altogether lovely. In Jesus' name, I pray. Amen.

Action Steps I Can Take Today

19. List some practical ways you can show love to others this week. Choose one and make a commitment to do it.

As you complete this study, remember this: You are born to be like Jesus.

> *And this is [our] prayer for you: That your love may abound more and more in knowledge and depth of insight, so that you may be able to discern what is best and may be pure and blameless until the day of Christ, filled with the fruit of righteousness that comes through Jesus Christ—to the glory and praise of God. Philippians 1:9-11*

Note:
1. C. I. Scofield, *Oxford NIV Scofield Bible* (New York: Oxford University Press, 1984), p. 1210.

What Is Aglow International?

From one nation to 135 worldwide...
From one fellowship to over 3,300...
From 100 women to more than 2 million...

Aglow International has experienced phenomenal growth since its inception 30 years ago. In 1967, four women from the state of Washington prayed for a way to reach out to other Christian women in simple fellowship, free from denominational boundaries.

The first meeting held in Seattle, Washington, USA, drew more than 100 women to a local hotel. From that modest beginning, Aglow International has become one of the largest intercultural, interdenominational women's organizations in the world.

Each month, Aglow touches the lives of an estimated two million women on six continents through local fellowship meetings, Bible studies, support groups, retreats, conferences and various outreaches. From the inner city to the upper echelons, from the woman next door to the corporate executive, Aglow seeks to minister to the felt needs of women around the world.

Christian women find Aglow a "safe place" to grow spiritually and begin to discover and use the gifts, talents and abilities God has given them. Aglow offers excellent leadership training and varied opportunities to develop those leadership skills.

Undergirding the evangelistic thrust of the ministry is an emphasis on prayer, which has led to an active prayer network linking six continents. The vast prayer power available through Aglow women around the world is being used by God to influence countless lives in families, communities, cities and nations.

Aglow's Mission Statement

Our mission is to lead women to Jesus Christ and provide opportunity for Christian women to grow in their faith and minister to others.

—⟩⟨⟨⟩—

Aglow's Continuing Focus...

- To reconcile woman to her womanhood as God designed. To strengthen and empower her to fulfill the unfolding plan of God as He brings restoration to the male/female relationship, which is the foundation of the home, the church and the community.
- To love women of all cultures with a special focus on Muslim women.
- To reach out to every strata of society, from inner cities to isolated outposts to our own neighborhoods, with very practical and tangible expressions of the love of Jesus.

—⟩⟨⟨⟩—

Gospel Light and Aglow International present an important new series of Bible studies for use in small groups. The first two studies in the Aglow Bible Study Series, **Shame: Thief of Intimacy** and **Keys to Contentment**, are available through Gospel Light. Look for these and others in the Aglow Bible Study Series including **Fashioned for Intimacy Study Guide**, companion to the book **Fashioned for Intimacy**, **Building Better Relationships** and **Choosing to Change**. For information about these and other outstanding Bible study resources from Aglow, call us at 1-800-793-8126.

Aglow Ministers In...

Albania, Angola, Anguilla, Antigua, Argentina, Aruba, Australia, Austria, Bahamas, Barbados, Belgium, Belize, Benin, Bermuda, Bolivia, Botswana, Brazil, British Virgin Islands, Bulgaria, Burkina Faso, Cameroon, Canada, Cayman Islands, Chile, China, Colombia, Congo (Rep. of), Congo (Dem. Rep. of), Costa Rica, Côte d'Ivoire, Cuba, Curaçao, Czech Republic, Denmark, Djibouti, Dominica, Dominican Republic, Ecuador, Egypt, El Salvador, England, Equatorial Guinea, Estonia, Ethiopia, Faroe Islands, Fiji, Finland, France, Gabon, the Gambia, Germany, Ghana, Greece, Grenada, Guam, Guatemala, Guinea, Guyana, Haiti, Honduras, Hungary, Iceland, India, Indonesia, Ireland, Israel, Jamaica, Japan, Kazakstan, Kenya, Korea, Kyrgyzstan, Latvia, Malawi, Malaysia, Mali, Mauritius, Mexico, Fed. States of Micronesia, Mongolia, Mozambique, Myanmar, Nepal, Netherlands, Papua New Guinea, New Zealand, Nicaragua, Niger, Nigeria, Norway, Oman, Pakistan, Panama, Peru, Philippines, Portugal, Puerto Rico, Romania, Russia, Rwanda, Samoa (American), Samoa (Western), Scotland, Senegal, Sierra Leone, Singapore, South Africa, Spain, Sri Lanka, St. Kitts, St. Lucia, St. Maarten, St. Vincent, Sudan, Suriname, Sweden, Switzerland, Tajikistan, Tanzania, Thailand, Togo, Tonga, Trinidad/ Tobago, Turks & Caicos Islands, Uganda, Ukraine, United States, U.S. Virgin Islands, Uruguay, Uzbekistan, Venezuela, Vietnam, Wales, Yugoslavia, Zambia, Zimbabwe, plus one extremely restricted 10/40 Window nation.

How do I find my nearest Aglow Fellowship? Call or write us at:

AGLOW
INTERNATIONAL

P.O. Box 1749, Edmonds, WA 98020-1749
Phone: (425) 775-7282 or 1-800-755-2456
Fax: (425) 778-9615   E-mail: aglow@aglow.org
Web site: http://www.aglow.org/

The Aglow Bible Study Series

Shame:
Thief of Intimacy
Marie Powers

Powers exposes the characteristics, contributors, and the cure for this emotion that affects women, knowingly or unknowingly, throughout the world.

Paperback • $6.99
ISBN 08307.21290
Available April 1998

Keys to
Contentment
Sharon A. Steele

Journey through this study of Paul's life and teachings in his letter to the Philippians and learn how to find the contentment and abundant, joyous life that Jesus promised.

Paperback • $6.99
ISBN 08307.21304
Available April 1998

Building Better
Relationships
Bobbie Yagel

Use the Scriptures to build successful relationships with your loved ones, friends and neighbors, and learn how to handle confrontations and know when and how to seek forgiveness.

Paperback • $6.99
ISBN 08307.21320
Available July 1998

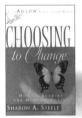

Choosing
to Change
Sharon A. Steele

Overcome rejection, guilt, fear, worry, discouragement and disobedience with the help of four essential steps to renew your mind and transform your life according to Christ.

Paperback • $6.99
ISBN 08307.21312
Available July 1998

Fashioned for Intimacy
Jane Hansen
with Marie Powers

Jane Hansen, international president of Aglow International, describes God's original design for men and women.

Hardcover • $17.99
ISBN 08307.20669
Available now

More titles in the *Aglow Bible Study Series* are coming soon: two in October 1998 and two in January 1999.

AGLOW.
INTERNATIONAL

Gospel Light

Ask for these resources at your local Christian Bookstore.

Let Jane Hansen Lead Your Next Study

Jane Hansen describes the true biblical relationship God yearns to have with each of us. Discover God's original plan for intimacy, and how men and women can be reconciled to Him and each other.

Video Study • UPC 607135.003649

"Fashioned for Intimacy will radically impact the Body of Christ! I highly recommend it to both men and women."
—*Dutch Sheets*
Pastor of Springs Harvest Fellowship
Colorado Springs, CO

"In a time when there is a massive assault coming against the family, resources like this one by Jane Hansen will help to turn the tide of the battle. This is must reading for men and women alike."
—*Rick Joyner*
Morningstar Publications and Ministries

Available at your local Christian bookstore.

Gospel Light